21

Story & Art by

Mizuho Kusanagi

Yona of the Dawn

Volume 21

CONTENTS

Yona of the Dawn

CHAPTER 118: GOING TOWARD YOU

I WAS JUST TOLD THAT LORD HOTSUMA'S FORT WAS ATTACKED BY INVADERS FROM KOHKA.
WHAT ?!
WHAT'S THEIR STATUS ?!
I DON'T KNOW. WE'VE BEEN ORDERED TO PREPARE FOR ATTACK TOO.
THEY'RE COMING HERE?!
DON'T WORRY.
LORD KUSHIBI'S TROOPS SHOULD ARRIVE SOON.
BE-SIDES ...

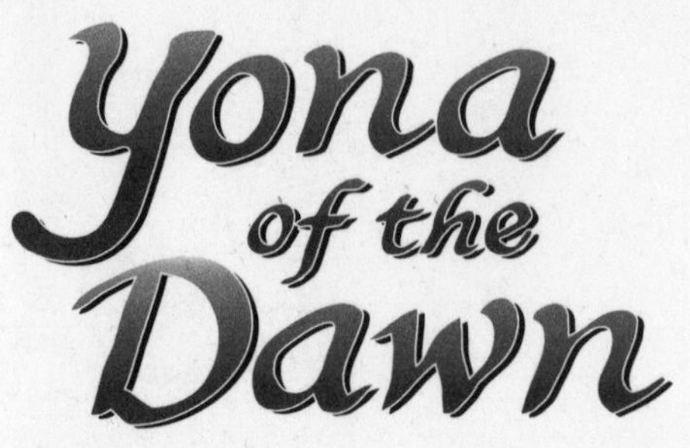
Yona of the Dawn

Hello! This is Mizuho Kusanagi. Thank you very much for picking up volume 21! The preorder special edition of volume 21 in Japan comes with an original anime DVD of the Zeno arc (Part 1). I'm really looking forward to it! 10/31 is the final day to preorder volume 22, which includes Part 2. Kaya makes an appearance too, so I hope you'll check it out! Preordering is the only way to get it, so make sure you do so at a bookstore or online!

The Nation of Sei arc wraps up in this volume. When I'm drawing, I usually struggle with something or other, but I got to draw the Wind Tribe and that was a lot of fun.

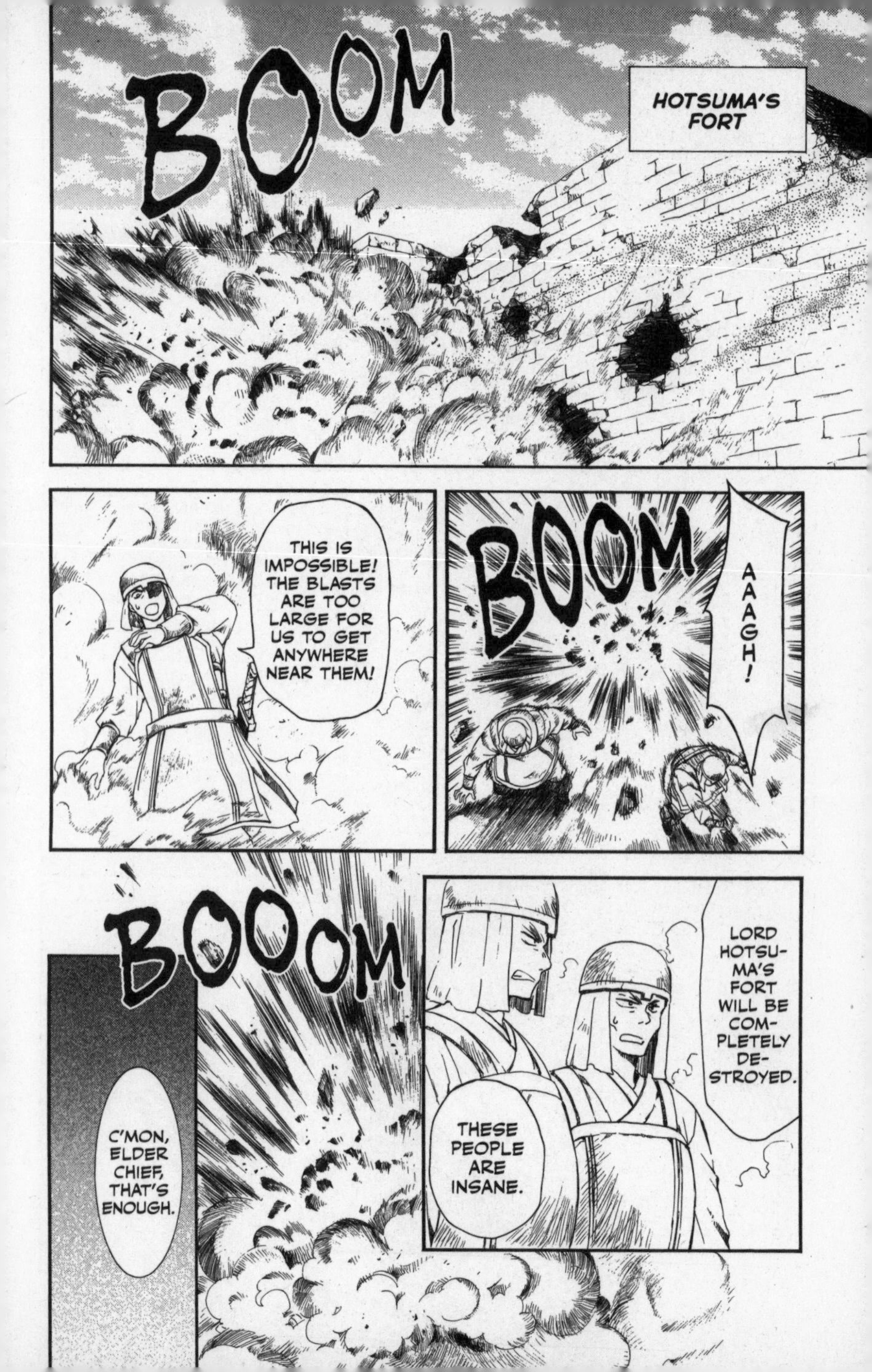
BOOM
HOTSUMA'S FORT
AAAGH!
BOOM
THIS IS IMPOSSIBLE! THE BLASTS ARE TOO LARGE FOR US TO GET ANYWHERE NEAR THEM!
LORD HOTSUMA'S FORT WILL BE COMPLETELY DESTROYED.
THESE PEOPLE ARE INSANE.
BOOOM
C'MON, ELDER CHIEF, THAT'S ENOUGH.

CAN WE JUST APPRECIATE BEING WITH LORD HAK INSTEAD OF TRYING TO KILL HIM?
IT'S *NOT* ENOUGH!
ARE YOU SAYING YOU LET HER HIGHNESS GET KIDNAPPED ON YOUR WATCH, YOU STUPID BRAT?!
FLING
LOOK, I'M NOT MAKING EXCUSES ...

KLANG
...BUT I'M NOT GONNA STAND HERE AND GET HIT WITH BOMBS.
BOOM
YOU'RE DEFLECTING WITH *MY* SPEAR.
IF YOU RUIN IT, I GET YOUR GLAIVE.
IT'S NOT HERE.
I didn't bring it.
FORGIVE HIM, ELDER CHIEF.
LORD HAK HAS BEEN PROTECTING HER HIGHNESS ALL BY HIMSELF.
NO.

NOT BY MY-SELF.
THE GUYS WITH ME ARE COMING TO GET HER BACK.
HUH? FRIENDS? YOU HAVE FRIENDS, LORD HAK?
Where are they?
I'M NOT SURE "FRIENDS" IS THE RIGHT WORD.
I SEE ...
YOU'VE FORGED A FAMILY YOU CAN TRUST.
THEY'RE NOT "FAMILY" EITHER.
WHOA! WHAT? I'M SO JEALOUS!

THAT'S GOOD TO HEAR.
LORD MUN-DEOK!
WHERE ARE YOU, LORD MUN-DEOK?
IT'S GEN-ERAL JU-DO.
HIDE, LORD HAK!
FWAP
Oof!
OVER HERE, JU-DO.

I HAVE A MESSAGE FROM HIS MAJESTY.
GENERAL JUNG-GI'S DAUGHTER ISN'T HERE.
HE'S HURRYING OVER TO KUSHIBI'S FORT, AND HE WANTS YOU TO MEET HIM THERE.
THE PRISONERS ARE SAFE IN OUR CUSTODY.
ALL RIGHT.
WE'LL HEAD THERE AT ONCE.

WE RELEASED ALL THE SLAVES.
I HEARD.
THE WATER TRIBE CHIEF WENT TO THE OTHER FORT TO SAVE RIRI.
I HEARD.
AND, AH...
KING SU-WON ...
...IS HERE.
...
I KNOW.

ARE YOU OKAY?
WE HAVE A JOB TO DO.
DROOPY-EYES IS TAKING TOO LONG TO CONTACT US.
WE'RE HEADING TO THE OTHER FORT TOO.

SKFF
SHHP
SHHP
...
GOOD-BYE.
RIRI...!

RUSTLE
THERE!
MUST BE HER.
!!
TCH.
THE CAPTAIN SENT US BACK OUT SINCE THERE WAS ANOTHER RUNAWAY.
I CAN'T BELIEVE SHE MADE IT ALL THIS WAY.
THESE ARE THE PEOPLE WHO TOOK HER?!
WHERE DID YOU TAKE RIRI?

NOW, NOW.
WE WON'T HURT HER.
WE WANT TO HEAR WHAT SHE HAS TO SAY.
COME WITH US, GIRLIE. YOU MUST BE EXHAUSTED.
THEY SAID SHE'D BE EXECUTED.
IF I'M CAPTURED, I CAN'T SAVE HER.
SKFF
DASH
HEY!
THAT STUPID—!

HMM...
THE YOUNG LADIES AREN'T IN SIGHT.
I WISH THE FOUR OF US COULD SENSE YONA'S WHEREABOUTS THE WAY WE DO WITH EACH OTHER.
THE CRIMSON DRAGON KING IS A NORMAL HUMAN.
I THINK THAT'S FINE.
RUSTLE
WELL, I SHOULD MAKE ONE MORE LEAP UP BEFORE IT GETS DARK.
COME ON.
HM?

I REMEMBER YOU MENTIONING THAT YOUR POWER GIVES YOU ABILITIES SIMILAR TO MINE AND GIJA'S.
CAN YOU USE SINHA'S POWER TOO?
ABOUT THAT...
So disap-pointing.
ZENO GOUGED OUT HIS OWN EYES ONCE BUT ONLY MANAGED TO MAKE THEM LESS FRAGILE.
I DON'T KNOW HOW TO RESPOND TO THAT.
BUT ZENO'S SIGHT WAS ALWAYS QUITE GOOD...
GREEN DRAGON, LET GO.
HUH?

LET GO RIGHT NOW!
VUP
ZENO ?!
GAH!
RUSTLE
HONESTLY ...

ZWOOOO
WHAM

W-
WHAT
WAS
THAT?!
IT
FELL
FROM
THE
SKY...
VOOOM

PLIP PLIP PLIP
A-AAGH!
ZENO?!
STEP AWAY FROM THE YOUNG LADY.
H-HE'S ALIVE...?!
SKRIK SKRIK
HIS WOUNDS ARE HEAL-ING...
THAT'S IMPOS-SIBLE—!

NO ONE COULD HEAL FROM THAT!
KLANG
!!

BAM
SORRY.
THE MORE HARM THESE CLOTHES TAKE, THE ANGRIER THE LAD WILL BE.

D...
DON'T MOVE!
IF YOU DO, THIS GIRL IS—
VOO

POW
WAM
GUH!
CRASH

YONA!
TMP
I'M GLAD YOU'RE SAFE.
WHERE IS RIRI?!
...
J...
JAEHA ...

WHAT DO WE DO...?
THEY... THEY TOOK RIRI...
THEY'RE GOING TO KILL HER!
I...
... COULDN'T PROTECT HER...

IT'S ALL RIGHT. WE'LL GO AFTER HER AS SOON AS POSSIBLE.
NNH...
YOU NEED TO GET SOME REST.
I'VE NEVER SEEN HER SO SHAKEN UP.
BUT OF COURSE SHE IS. SHE'S STILL ONLY 16.
SHE HAS LIMITS, AND SHE'S REACHED THEM.
SWFF
YOU DID WELL, YOUNG LADY.
GREEN DRAGON, CARRY THE YOUNG LADY ON YOUR BACK.
ZENO WILL RUN.

YONA, IF YOU NEED WATER, WE CAN FIND SOME.
SWOOSH
NO. KEEP GOING.
YOUR LEGS...
...ARE WONDERFUL.
I WISH I COULD...
...FLY RIGHT TO...
...THE PEOPLE I LOVE.

I'LL SERVE AS YOUR LEGS...
...UNTIL YOU NO LONGER ...
... HAVE USE FOR ME.

TROMP
TROMP
TROMP
TROMP
TROMP
TROMP
TROMP
CHAPTER 118 / THE END

CHAPTER 119:
KUSHIBI'S FORT

THIS IS KUSHIBI'S FORT, ISN'T IT?
THE SLAVES AND SOL-DIERS...
...AREN'T HERE.
WHERE IS LADY RIRI?
GEN-ERAL JUNG-GI.

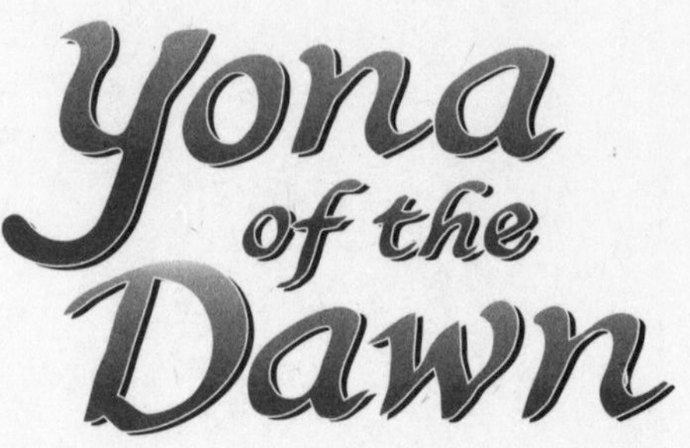
Yona of the Dawn

YOUR MAJ- ESTY?
THEY BUILT THEM- SELVES A NICE LITTLE PLACE HERE, I SEE.
IT WOULD SEEM THEY ANTICIPATED OUR ARRIVAL.
YES, BUT LET'S SEE WHAT'S INSIDE.
WHERE'D THE PRISON- ERS GO?

YOU THINK HER HIGH-NESS WAS HERE TOO?
PROB-ABLY.
DID YOU FIND ANY-ONE?
CAN'T SAY WE HAVE.
DO YOU SUPPOSE ALL THESE THINGS BELONG TO THE CAPTURED PEOPLE?
SEEMS LIKE IT.

WE SHOULD PACK THIS ALL UP TO BE RETURNED TO THE OWNERS.
Some of these things look valuable.
KLAK
JOLT
YOUR MAJ-ESTY.
WHAT'S THE MATTER?

IT'S NOTH-ING.
HAVE YOU FOUND ANYONE?
THERE DOESN'T SEEM TO BE ANYONE IN THIS FORT. I'D LIKE PERMISSION TO EXPLORE FURTHER.
OF COURSE.
I'LL GO WITH YOU.
WE'LL BE NEAR THE FORT SOON.

TROMP TROMP
I DON'T SEE RIRI ANYWHERE.
SHE'S NOT WITH THIS SQUAD.
SHE COULD BE FARTHER UP.
LET'S HURRY.
YEAH.
HFF
IT'LL BE ALL RIGHT.
I CAN SENSE GIJA AND THE OTHERS NEARBY.
HAK'S WITH THEM TOO.
WE WON'T LET THEM KILL HER.
RIGHT!

RIRI...
PLEASE BE SAFE!
GET IN LINE!
THEY'RE ASSEMBLING ALL THE SLAVES IN THE FORT'S CENTER. WHAT FOR?
GRAB
!
LORD KUSHIBI WILL BE ARRIVING SOON.
KNEEL BEFORE HIM.
KUSHIBI?
KLAT KLAT

KUSHIBI... THE MOST POWERFUL PERSON IN ALL OF SEI!
TROMP
TROMP
TROMP
TROMP
BRING THE RUNAWAY OUT FOR HER EXECUTION.

AN EXECUTION...?
WOBBLE
LADY RIRI!
SHUP
DON'T MOVE.

NOT ONE STEP...
SHA
...UNLESS YOU WANT TO BE EXECUTED WITH HER.
NATURALLY. SHE TRIED TO ESCAPE.
THAT GIRL'S GOING TO BE KILLED RIGHT HERE?!
LADY RIRI'S BY HERSELF?! WHERE'S LADY YONA?!
WHAT A HASSLE. GET STARTED, WILL YOU?
I'M TERRIBLY SORRY, MY LORD.
IT'S JUST... SOME PEOPLE FROM KOHKA HAVE INVADED THE FORT...
I'VE HEARD, YES.
THEY BROUGHT HOTSUMA'S FORT DOWN WITH JUST A FEW MEN.
THEY PROBABLY CAME FOR THE SLAVES. I IMAGINE THEY'RE RELATIVES OR SOMETHING.

HOTSUMA'S REPUTATION IS RUINED.
I'LL BEHEAD THE INVADERS.
THEIR TIMING COULDN'T BE BETTER.
WE'LL GIVE THEM A WARM WELCOME TO THE EXECUTION GROUNDS.
THEY CAN'T TOUCH US.
WE DETERMINE WHETHER THESE SLAVES LIVE OR DIE.

HOW ODD.
I DON'T FEEL SCARED AT ALL.
MOSTLY I'M SO FURIOUS AT THAT ARROGANT MAN OVER THERE AND HIS PLEASED SMIRK...
...THAT IT'S MAKING ME DIZZY.
I WONDER IF YONA'S ALL RIGHT...
COME FORWARD, CRIMINAL.

WUMP
Agh!
SHNK
SWFF
Y...
YOU FILTH!
?!
AYURA?!

About turning the Zeno arc into an OAD... I had an offer to create two OADs, so my editor and I discussed which storyline to do. I initially asked Pierrot to do the contents of volumes 17 and 18. But a 30-minute anime can only cover about two 30-page chapters of the manga, so cramming volumes 17 and 18 into two episodes would be quite difficult. I was prepared to make it a summary, but Pierrot suggested that it might be better to animate Zeno's past from volume 18, and we decided to go with that. I never expected to see Zeno's past animated, so I'm very happy.

I'm glad I put so much effort into that storyline!

DON'T, AYURA!
RUN!
IF YOU DIE...
...I...!
WHEEZE
WHAT ARE YOU DOING? HURRY AND KILL HER.
BUT THIS WOMAN ...
IF YOU'RE GOING TO KILL ME, JUST DO IT!

BEFORE I ESCAPED, I STABBED A SOLDIER!
HE DESERVED IT! HE WAS TRYING TO PUNISH ME FOR NO REASON!
AYURA, PLEASE ...!
I STABBED HIM FROM BEHIND!
I'M GIVING YOU AN OPENING!
I DIDN'T EX-PECT ...
GET AWAY! HURRY!
...SEI SOLDERS TO BE SO WEAK AND PATHETIC!
LADY RIRI...!

YOU WITCH!
KILL ME IF YOU CAN, YOU COWARDS!
SHUT UP!
SLAP
LADY RIRI!
GRAB

SO YOU'RE THE ONE... ...WHO KILLED HIM.
YOU ASKED FOR DEATH, YOU'LL GET IT.
AYURA...
GOOD-BYE.
THANK YOU FOR COMING TO SAVE ME.
LADY RIRI!!

WHAT'S THE MATTER, YOUR MAJ-ESTY?
DID YOU... HEAR SOME-THING?
...?
AH!
THUK
THUK
THUK
THUK
STAY BACK!
DON'T MOVE, INTRUD-ERS.

THERE ARE 100 ARROWS AIMED AT YOU.
WELCOME TO MY FORT.
YOU'VE BEEN LED HERE.
A SPIRITED YOUNG GIRL IS ABOUT TO DIE.
WHY DON'T YOU COME WATCH?

LADY RIRI ?!
TMP TMP
THERE.
THERE'RE SO MANY SOLDIERS!
I DIDN'T KNOW THERE WAS AN OPEN SPACE IN THE FORT'S CENTER...

RIRI IS IN DANGER.
WHAT'S GOING ON?! WHERE'S YONA?
I DON'T SENSE JAEHA AND ZENO, EITHER.
LET'S GO.
AAAGH!
BOOM
WHAT WAS THAT?!

W-WE DON'T KNOW. THERE ARE MORE INVADERS COMING FROM A DIFFERENT DIRECTION!
BOOM
PUT THEM DOWN. I'VE BROUGHT 1,000 SOLDIERS FOR JUST SUCH AN EVENTUALITY!
TAE-U, LOOK.
AAAGH!
POW
GAAH!

LADY RIRI!
ZLISH
AYURA!!
FWP
SHA

SLISH
KLAT

A PATHETIC SHOT LIKE THAT WON'T KILL OUR CHIEF.
DON'T PROVOKE THEM, IDIOT.
You moved first, Tae-u.
HE DOES HAVE A POINT.
WE'VE COME TO GET LADY RIRI BACK.
WE WERE POLITELY INVITED IN...
...BUT I DOUBT KUSHIBI REALIZES THAT...

CHAPTER 119 / THE END

DON'T MOVE, INTRUDERS!
KRIK

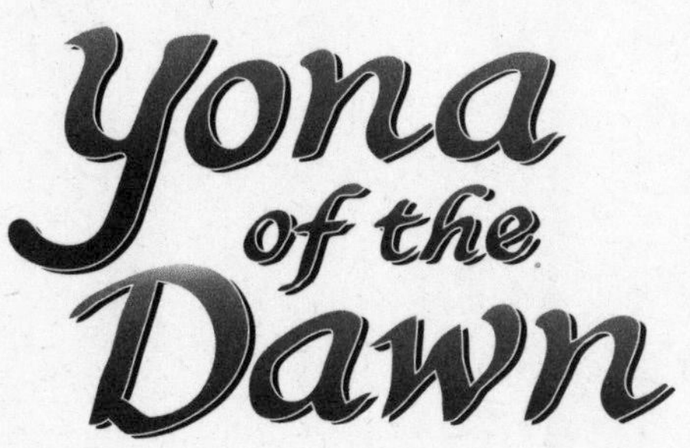
Yona of the Dawn

LOOSE THE AR-ROWS!
FWP
FWP
YOUR MAJ-ESTY ... PLEASE KEEP BACK!
RAMARU, MY BOW.
AT ONCE!

CHAPTER 120:
REACHING YOU
KILL THE INTRUD-ERS!

SL
SH
KR
AK
GENERAL TAE-U, HANDLE THINGS ABOVE.
GENERAL GEUN-TAE, YOU GET LADY RIRI.
ELDER CHIEF MUN-DEOK, PLEASE TAKE CARE OF THE PRISONERS.
...
HYEONG-DAE!

HM?!
HYEONG-DAE IS ON IT!
LOOK, HE'S CLIMBING UP!
At full speed!
TAK TAK TAK TAK TAK
TAK TAK TAK TAK TAK
SHOOT HIM!
FW
LEAP
SH

THMP
!
ACK! I WASN'T EXPECTING SO MANY OF YOU.
YOU LITTLE—
HURRY UP, TAE-U!
UGH...
Can't match his pace
RIGHT. LET'S DO THIS.
GOT IT, YOUNG CHIEF.

MAJESTY.
PLEASE ALLOW ME TO GO HELP RESCUE LADY RIRI AND AYURA.
ALL RIGHT, YOU DO THAT.
THAT HAIRPIN WAS AMONG THE PRISONERS' POSSESSIONS.
WAS YONA BROUGHT HERE AS A SLAVE TOO?
GENERAL JU-DO, ASSIST GENERAL GEUN-TAE.
I'M STAYING PUT.
I'LL BE FINE. I WON'T BE ON THE FRONT LINES.
I SAW THE THUNDER BEAST OVER THERE.
NOTHING IN THE WORLD SCARES ME MORE THAN HIM.

KRAK
GUH!
WHAM
WHITE SNAKE.
HM?
WHERE ARE DROOPY-EYES AND ZENO?!
I'M NOT SURE. THEY'RE PROBABLY NOT IN THE IMMEDIATE VICINITY.
I SEE.
IS HER HIGHNESS SOME-WHERE ELSE, THEN?

IT'LL BE ALL RIGHT.
I CAN LEAVE IT TO THEM.
WHITE SNAKE, SINHA, I'M GOING AFTER RIRI.
TAKE CARE OF THIS AREA.
OF COURSE. BUT YOU'RE UNARMED.
SO ARE YOU.
Hm?!
LET'S STOP ALL THIS NON-SENSE...
...AND GET TO HER HIGH-NESS.
DASH
YAAAH!

GRAB
UHN ...
GRP
YANK
AGH!
I'LL JUST TAKE THIS OFF YOUR HANDS.

THOK
SWING
AAGH!
LORD KUSHI-BI!
TMP

IT'S TOO DANGER-OUS HERE. YOU NEED TO GET TO SOME-PLACE SAFE!
WHY CAN'T YOU LOT KILL THIS FEW MEN?
JUST HURRY UP AND HANG THE GIRL!
SOME OTHER SLAVES TOO!
WHP
WE'VE GOT PLENTY OF HOSTAGES.
KILL THEM ONE BY ONE AS A WARNING!
AAAGH!

MOVE!
AAAH!
FORGIVE ME.
WHY ARE YOU DRAGGING PEOPLE HERE?!
THEY WEREN'T INVOLVED!
WE'VE BEEN ORDERED TO HANG THEM ONCE WE'RE DONE WITH YOU.
NO!
NO, PLEASE!
I DON'T WANT TO DIE!

?!
UGH!
AAAAAH!

I WON'T LIE DOWN AND DIE WITHOUT A FIGHT!
Y...
YOU ...!
WHY ARE YOU ALL JUST STANDING THERE?!
IF YOU WANT TO LIVE...
...START FIGHTING BACK!

TAKE THAT!
AH!
THUD
!
STAGGER
LADY RIRI!!
RIRI!!
TCH!
HUH...?

AM I IMAGINING THINGS? I THOUGHT I HEARD...
...TETRA AND MY FATHER.
THAT CAN'T BE.
TETRA I COULD BELIEVE...
...BUT FATHER WOULD NEVER...
...COME HERE...
MOVE ASIDE!
SLASH
CURSE IT ALL!
AH!
JAEHA ...!

OH!
JAEHA, OVER THERE!
RIRI!
STOP THEM!
SOME-ONE...
...SAVE RIRI!

Hana to Yume issue 18, which goes on sale the same time as this graphic novel in Japan (8/20), comes with a drama CD. It contains chapters 109 and 110 from volume 19 as well as the short bonus chapter from volume 18. You'll get to hear Riri, Ayura and Tetra!!
The cast members are...
Riri → Aoi Yuuki
Ayura → Himika Akaneya
Tetra → Mamika Noto
They played their roles beautifully with their adorable voices. ✧✧ (Much respect.)
Yona was also incredibly cute. This time, we also hear Su-won's side of the story, so it's an unbelievably splendid CD. There are some conversations between Yona and her friends that you can only hear on this CD, so check it out. ✧✧

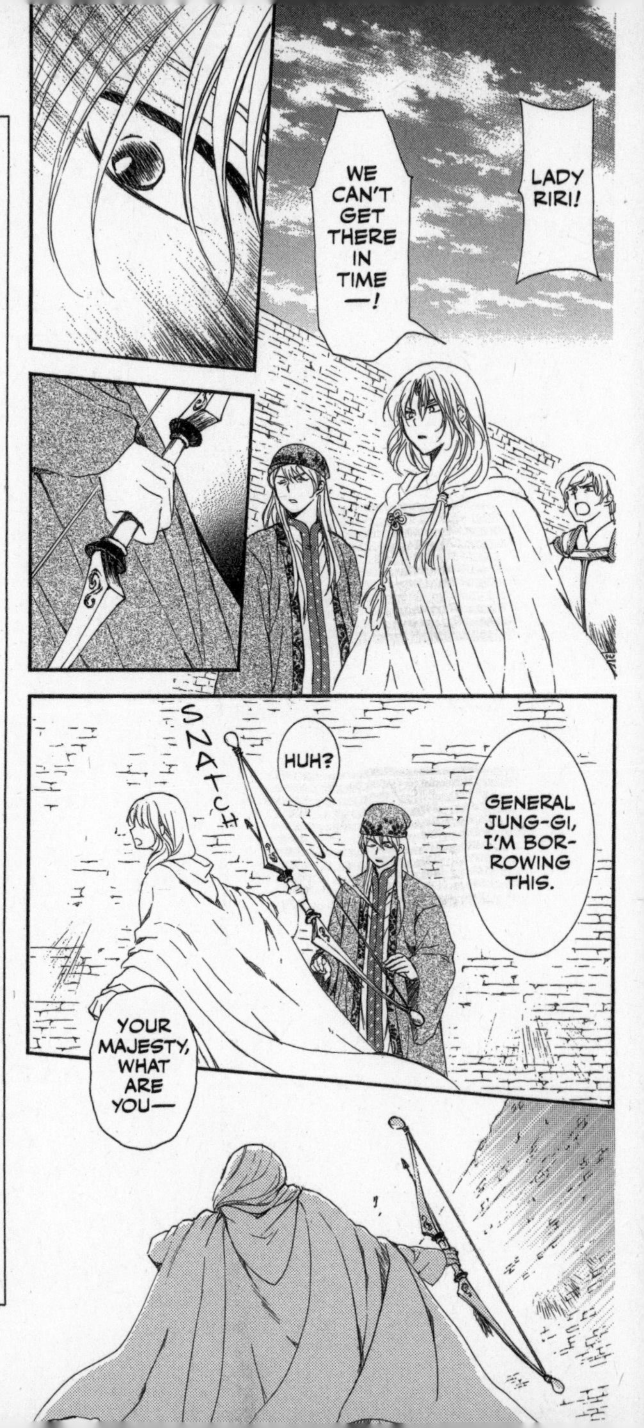

A BOW ...
...YOUR MAJ-ESTY ?!
IT'S AN IMPOS-SIBLE SHOT!
AND EVEN IF YOU MAKE IT...
I CAN MAKE IT—JUST BARELY.

THE TROUBLE IS...
...SOME-ONE NEEDS TO CATCH HER.
!
SOME-ONE...
TH-THMP
SOME-ONE...!
TH-THMP

HANG HER!

FW
P
SH
SN IK

VWUP

SKFFF

Hff...
Hff...
Phew...

KLAK
W-WHAT?
I couldn't see it!
WHAT HAP-PENED?
HAK SAVED RIRI...
AH!
TMP

YONA, DID YOU SEE?
HAK SAVED RIRI.
YONA ...?
ARE YOU OKAY?
CHAPTER 120 / THE END

I WAS...
...MESMERIZED.
HAK...
SU-WON...
IF YOU TWO HAD WOUND UP ON THE SAME SIDE...
...WOULD THERE BE ANY LIMIT TO WHAT YOU COULD ACCOMPLISH?
SO...
...WHY...
...DID THINGS ...

CHAPTER 121: SINCE THAT DAY

YONA ...
I-I'M FINE.
I'M SO GLAD RIRI IS SAFE.
YONA!
YUN ...!
YOU'RE ALL RIGHT! THANK GOODNESS...!
SORRY FOR MAKING YOU WORRY.

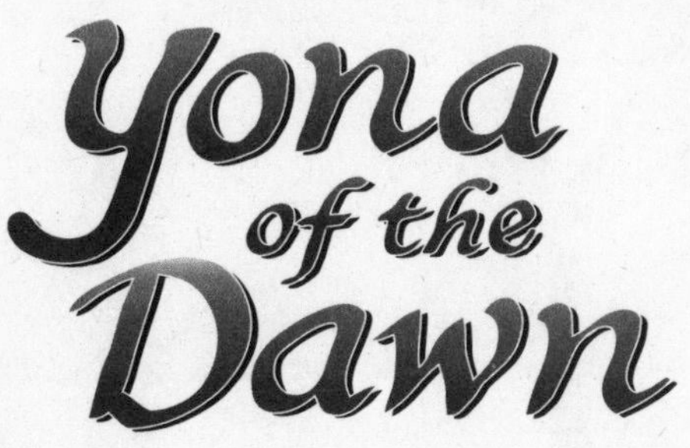
Yona of the Dawn

YUN, LOOK AFTER YONA.
I'M GOING TO HELP THEM FIGHT.
WHERE'S ZENO?
HE'LL BE ALONG.
JAEHA.
I...
...WANT TO GO TO HAK RIGHT NOW.
SU-WON WAS SO CLOSE, AND...
AND HAK...
I'M WOR-RIED.
ALL RIGHT.

I'LL BRING HAK STRAIGHT TO YOU.
YOU'RE BONE-TIRED. IT'D BE TOO RISKY...
...FOR YOU TO WADE INTO THAT CHAOS.
YEAH.
THAT'S TRUE.
PLEASE BE CAREFUL TOO, JAEHA.
THANK YOU SO MUCH...
...FOR COMING TO SAVE ME.

Phew.
SHE'S ALIVE.
DON'T MOVE.
CHAK
YOU THINK YOU SAVED HER? THINK AGAIN.
I CAN'T BELIEVE YOU CAME HERE UNARMED.

SLASH
GAAH!
YOU...
SLASH
URK...

SHE'S UNCONSCIOUS?
YEAH.
I SEE.
MURMUR
MURMUR...

There was a stage show of Yona of the Dawn back in March 2016. ✧✧ I was excited to see how my comic would translate to the stage! Yona and her friends, Su-won, Riri and Riri's attendants are all so lively and cute! Hyo and his gang are so suspicious! I was completely hooked on the charm of watching a live stage show!! It was all so electric with everyone's desire to entertain the audience, and I was delighted. Seeing how hard the actors worked, even after the show ended, made me want to go see other shows. To everyone involved, thank you!

KILL THEM!
EVERY LAST ONE!
AT ONCE!
HEAD TO THE EXE-CUTION PLAT-FORM!
ALL SOL-DIERS, HEAD THERE!
SHUP

SLASH
AAAGH!
SKFF

Y...
YOU OLD MAN...
POW
YAGH!

LADY RIRI!
IT'S OKAY. SHE'S ALIVE.
TAKE CARE OF HER.
THANK YOU SO MUCH!
SKFF
YOU WON'T GET AWAY!
THOK THOK THOK THOK
GUH ...

FWP
HEY.
GRP
WHOEVER YOU ARE, YOU UN-FAMILIAR KID...
THANK YOU FOR SAVING JUNG-GI'S DAUGHTER.
SLASH
OH, WHAT'S THAT?
SHE'S SOME BIG SHOT'S DAUGHTER? GUESS I SHOULD EXPECT REWARD MONEY.
HAVE SOME CANDY.
YOU SHOULD SCRAM BEFORE YOU GET CAUGHT UP IN THIS, SLAVE.
SLISH
MNCH
YOU'RE NOT WRONG.

MNCH
MNCH
TROUBLE IS, WE'RE SURROUNDED.
LOOKS THAT WAY.
LET'S GET THIS DONE.
SWP
GAAH!
SHUNK
SHUNK
FMP
HEY.

IT'S BEEN A WHILE.
DROOPY-EYES.
SWP
KRAK
I SEE THINGS HAVE GOTTEN EXCITING AROUND HERE.
ALSO, SHE'S FINE.
LET'S GET HER AND RIRI OUT OF HERE AND—
HUG

SHUK
AAGH!
IT'S A GREETING.
HUH?
What did I just experience?
Yun, I need a comeback!
YONA SAYS SHE WANTS TO SEE YOU RIGHT AWAY.
LIAR.
SLASH
HE LIKES TO FEED THE "UNREQUITED" PART OF HIS LOVE, HMM?

QUIVER
QUIVER
HEY... IS ANY-ONE...
...HERE?

YES, LORD KUSHIBI.
SUDDENLY I'M... SEEING MORE CLEARLY.
ALL THE SOLDIERS WHO WERE JUST HERE...
WHERE DID THEY GO...?
WAS I...
...OPERATING UNDER...
...SOME HUGE DELUSION?
WHAT ARE...
...SUCH MONSTROUSLY STRONG PEOPLE...
...DOING HERE?

OOOOo

Zw
WHAT HAVE I...
...INVITED IN?

LORD KUSHIBI ...URK!
THOK
CHAK
STAY RIGHT THERE.
WHO ARE THEY...?
...
YOU'RE LORD KUSHIBI, AREN'T YOU?
INDEED.
I AM...
...KUSHIBI.

AND WHO...
...MIGHT YOU BE?
THE RULER OF KOHKA.
MY NAME IS SU-WON.

THE...
THE RULER...?
HA...
THAT'S RIDICULOUS.
WHY WOULD A KING COME HERE WITH SO FEW MEN?
"FEW" ...?
FOUR GENERALS OF KOHKA STAND WITH ME.
SURELY THAT IS SUFFICIENT?

THAT'S EVEN MORE UNTHINKABLE!
WHY ARE ALL OF YOU HERE?
THE GIRL YOU NEARLY EXECUTED IS THE DAUGHTER OF THE WATER TRIBE CHIEF.
THAT GIRL ...?
WHAT'S MORE, I KNOW HER PERSONALLY...
...AND VALUE HER HIGHLY. YOU ABDUCTED AND TRIED TO KILL HER.
IF I CUT OFF YOUR HEAD HERE AND NOW...
...I'M SURE YOU ...
NO.
I'M SURE THIS *NATION* ...

...WOULD CONSIDER IT FAIR.
A-ALL RIGHT.
THIS MAN...
...IS REALLY...
I'LL DO WHATEVER YOU WANT.
...KOHKA'S RULER...
I SEE.
IN THAT CASE, DISMANTLE THIS FORT...
...AND FREE EVERY LAST PERSON YOU ABDUCTED FROM THE WATER TRIBE.
Y-YES.

WE'LL MEET WITH KING KAZAGUMO IN A WHILE TO WORK OUT THE DETAILS.
UNTIL THEN, YOU WILL COME TO KOHKA.
IT'S OVER.
ALL BECAUSE I BROUGHT THAT GIRL HERE...
SEI, MY NATION...
BEAR IN MIND THAT...
...WILL BECOME A SUBJECT OF KOHKA.
...A HANDFUL OF OUR WARRIORS TOOK DOWN A THOUSAND OF YOURS.

WHAT YOU SAW TODAY...
...WAS MERELY A FRACTION OF KOHKA'S STRENGTH.

DASH

HOLD ON.
ARE YOU GOING TO PERMIT THAT MAN TO WALK OUT OF HERE?
CHAPTER 121 / THE END

CHAPTER 122: BY YOUR SIDE

ARE YOU GOING TO PERMIT THAT MAN TO WALK OUT OF HERE?
YOU SAID THAT...
...YOU'D CUT HIM DOWN NEXT TIME YOU SAW HIM.

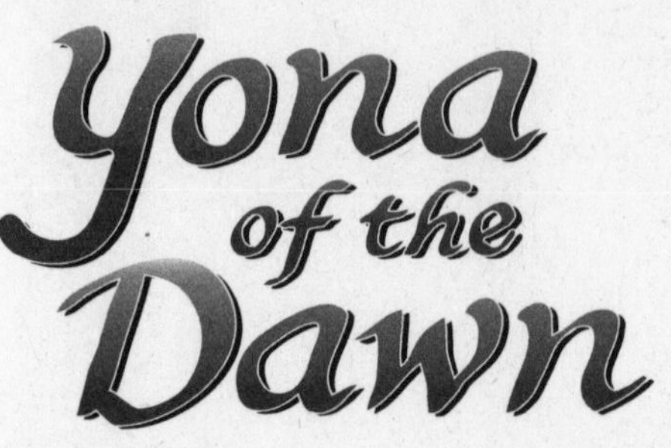
Yona of the Dawn

CHAK
SH
NK
GEN-
ERAL
JU-DO!
HEY.

THE BATTLE'S OVER.
WHY ARE YOU STILL THIRSTY FOR BLOOD?
WHY ARE *YOU* NOT THINKING STRAIGHT?
THE MAN WE SHOULD BE MOST WARY OF...
...IS *RIGHT THERE.*
...

IF YOU'RE NOT HELPING ME, THEN SHUT YOUR MOUTH.
GENERAL JUNG-GI'S DAUGHTER HAS NOTHING TO DO WITH THIS.
THAT'S NOT TRUE.
HE JUST HELPED US SAVE RIRI.
I UNDER-STAND HOW YOU FEEL, BUT FOR TODAY, AT LEAST...
IF HE HADN'T SAVED RIRI, SHE'D BE—
YOU CLEARLY DON'T GRASP ...
...HOW TERRIFY-ING THE THUNDER BEAST IS!

SOMEDAY HE'LL BE A THREAT TO HIS MAJESTY'S LIFE!
BEFORE THAT CAN HAPPEN ...
...I'LL DO ALL I CAN TO KILL HIM!
JUST BECAUSE WE CO-OPERATED TODAY...
GEN-ERAL JU-DO.

STAND DOWN.
YOU STILL HAVEN'T GOTTEN PAST YOUR FEELINGS ?!
THAT'S NOT IT.
PAY AT-TENTION TO HOW MUCH...
...ANI-MOSITY IS BEING AIMED AT YOU.

THE FIVE TRIBES ARE ON THE VERGE OF BEING UNITED.
MAKING AN ENEMY OF THE WIND TRIBE WOULD NOT BE WISE.
BE-SIDES ...

THEN THERE'S KUSHIBI AND THE SEI SOLDIERS.
WE NEED TO DEAL WITH THEM FIRST.
...
...IF WE TRY TO FIGHT *THEM* HEAD-ON...
...WE WON'T GET OUT OF HERE ALIVE.

AND WHO EXACTLY ARE THEY?
THE FOUR DRAGON WARRIORS, EVIDENTLY.
HUH?
CLENCH

I'M FINE, OKAY?
OKAY.

YONA... THOSE PEOPLE ARE LOOKING AT US.
HMM?
MUN-DEOK!
...
THEY WERE BROUGHT HERE TO RESCUE RIRI.

JU—
TMP TMP TMP TMP TMP TMP

ZOOOOOOM!
FWAM
AHH!
YOUR MAJ-ESTY?!
OWW ...
HUH? ZENO OVER-SHOT.

DON'T MOVE!
OH.
EVERY-THING'S FINE, GENERAL.
WAIT, YOU'RE...
OH, IT'S THE KING.
WHY ARE YOU HERE?
PAT PAT
TO SAVE LADY RIRI.
HMM...
LOOKS LIKE KOHKA HAS SEI IN THE PALM OF ITS HAND WITHOUT A SINGLE CASUALTY.

ARE YOU ONE OF THE FOUR DRAG-ONS?
HOW DO YOU—
THE WHITE DRAGON TOLD ME.
OH.
YOU'RE RIGHT.
Yep.
I SEE.
DO YOU WANT THE FOUR DRAGON WARRIORS?
HUH?
NO, NOT AT ALL.

WELL, ZENO'S OFF NOW.
OH...
BYE, NOW ...
... YOUNG KING.

ZENO!
ZENO is Back...
...YOUNG LADY!
ZENO! YOU'RE ALL BLOODY!
You were being reckless again.
AH HA HA...
GOOD WORK, ZENO.
I'M GLAD TO SEE YOU!
ZENO FLEW IN TO SAVE ME WHEN I WAS IN DANGER.
I'D CALL THAT FALLING, NOT FLYING.
ZENO TRIED HARD TO SPARE HIS CLOTHES—

HUG
HUH?
OH?
HUH?
WHAT'S THIS ABOUT, NOW?!
A RE-WARD.
HA HA! A REWARD?
YAY!
BUT ZENO CAN'T BREATHE.
THANK GOODNESS.
HAK...
...HAS CALMED DOWN.

I'M...
...FINE NOW.
YOU DON'T NEED TO CRY...
... GIJA.
BUT... BUT YOUR HIGH-NESS...
YOU'RE BRUISED ALL OVER...!
THANK YOU.
SORRY FOR WOR-RYING YOU.
I-I... DIDN'T HELP...

ALL RIGHT, GIJA, DRY THOSE TEARS AND HAVE SOME-THING TO EAT.
ZENO, STOP LAZING ABOUT AND SIT UP.
WHEN THE YOUNG FELLOW HUGGED ZENO, ZENO HEARD SOME BONES CRACK.
I KNOW THE FEEL-ING!
I heard my bones crunch.
HUH? YOU GOT A HUG TOO, JAEHA?
I DID. I WONDER WHY HE'S SUDDENLY SO AFFEC-TIONATE.
HAK DID THAT ...?
How unusual.
...

HAK, YONA WANTS YOU TO HUG HER TOO!
HUH?
HEY ...!
JAEHA!
WHY... WHY WOULD YOU THINK THAT?!
IT'S WRITTEN ALL OVER YOUR FACE.
I didn't say that!
IT IS NOT!
WHAT?
SHUP SHUP
LISTEN, YONA WANTS —
JAEHA!
D-DON'T ...

WHOA...
WHY DO I SUDDENLY FEEL LIKE MY WHOLE HEART'S BEING WRENCHED?
BUT...

...AS LONG AS SHE'LL LET ME SEE HER SMILE...
...I...
...COULDN'T WISH...
...FOR ANYTHING MORE.
ALL RIGHT. I'LL CUT IT OUT.
NOW SLEEP. YOU MUST BE EX-HAUSTED.

OKAY ...
SUCH CHEERFUL SOUNDS...
BEING ABLE TO HEAR EVERYONE...
...LETS ME RELAX.
I'M...
...BACK NOW.

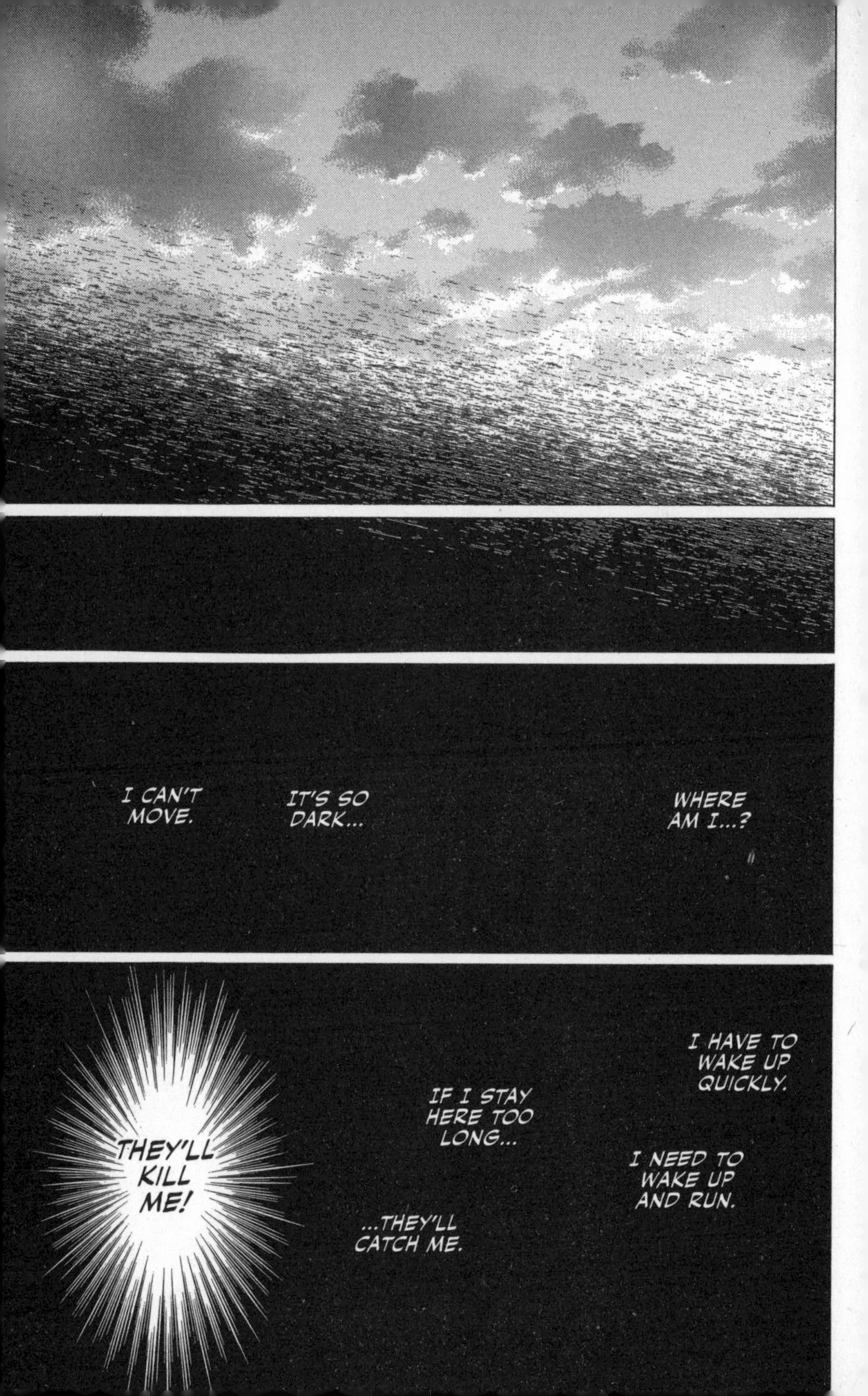
WHERE AM I...?
IT'S SO DARK...
I CAN'T MOVE.
I HAVE TO WAKE UP QUICKLY.
I NEED TO WAKE UP AND RUN.
IF I STAY HERE TOO LONG...
...THEY'LL CATCH ME.
THEY'LL KILL ME!

GASP
THAT'S RIGHT.
I'M SAFE NOW.
The neighboring tent

I SHOULD...
...GO SEE RIRI.
Whew...
HUH?
WHERE'S HAK?
How They Went About Becoming Slaves
All right, we're going to Sei for an undercover investigation. I call it "Operation Attract Slavers."
No one's going to kidnap a man with such a huge weapon or someone wearing a mask. Sinha's sword is just barely passable.
So do I have to leave my concealed weapons?
STRIP
They wouldn't want a weirdo who enjoys stripping, either.
...
Guess I can't tell you to remove your arm.
And so, Hak's glaive and Sinha's mask were left behind.

RUSTLE
PRIN-CESS?
WHAT ARE YOU DOING UP THIS LATE?
SAME TO YOU.
WE WERE RUNNING LOW ON FIREWOOD, SO I WAS GETTING MORE.
GO GET SOME SLEEP.
I WON'T BE LONG.

AH... PRIN- CESS?
IS YOUR LEG HURTING?
...
HAK ...

I...
...WANT TO TOUCH YOU.

CAN I...
...STAY HERE WITH YOU?
CHAPTER 122 / THE END

CHAPTER 123: INEXPRESSIBLE FEELINGS

A special thanks!
My assistants → Mikorun, C.F., Ryo, Ryo Sakura, Oka, Awafuji, Eika and my little sister...
My editor Tokushige, my previous editors and the *Hana to Yume* editorial office...
Everyone who's involved in creating and selling Yona-related merchandise...
My beloved family and friends who've always supported me...
And you, for reading this!
Thank you so very much! This series is getting long, but I'll keep doing my best, and I hope you'll keep reading!

BLUSH
WHAT AM I SAYING?!
UH...
NO...
YOU DIDN'T HEAR THAT!
I-I'M GOING BACK TO BED.
TRIP
EEP!

SHA
HAK...
...
YOU DON'T SEEM FEVER-ISH.
MAYBE I'M THE ONE WITH A FEVER...?
AM I HEARING THINGS?
THE RESULT OF HAVING ONE-SIDED FEELINGS FOR MANY YEARS

MAYBE ...
...HE DIDN'T REALLY HEAR ME?
Phew
← Pondering
THAT WAS CLOSE. IF HE'D HEARD, HE'D TEASE ME FOR SURE.
BUT IT'S BEEN SO LONG SINCE WE'VE BEEN TOGETHER ...
I, UM... I CAN'T SLEEP. CAN WE TALK FOR A WHILE?
SURE.
I SEE. SHE JUST WANTS TO TALK TO SETTLE HER MIND DOWN.
GUESS I REALLY WAS HEARING THINGS.
SHALL WE SIT OVER THERE?
OKAY ...
WHUP

YOUR HIGH-NESS?
I...
I JUST REALIZED...
...I HAVEN'T BATHED IN A WHILE!
MORTIFIED
I'VE CHANGED MY CLOTHES...
...AND WIPED MYSELF DOWN WITH A CLOTH...
...BUT I HAVEN'T WASHED MY HAIR.
I PROBABLY SMELL AWFUL!
PRIN-CESS?
WHAT'S WRONG?
SHA
RETREAT

SCUTTLE
YOUR HIGH—
ZWOOM
Y—
SHA SHA SHA SHA SHA SHA
FWOOOSH

WHAT'S THE PROBLEM?! YOU SAID YOU WANTED TO TALK, SO I WAS JUST GOING TO TAKE YOUR HAND!
AM I NOT ALLOWED NEAR YOU ANYMORE ?!
True feelings bursting out
S...
SORRY ...
AND HOW WERE YOU MOVING FASTER THAN ME?!
You were as fast as Hyeong-dae!
SHEER DETER-MINA-TION!
WELL? IS THIS FAR ENOUGH AWAY FOR YOU?
WHAT'S THIS ABOUT? THE STUFF PU-KYU STASHES IN HER CHEEK POUCHES?
That sounds like a fun topic, but...
N-NO, UM...
I'D LIKE TO...
...BE CLOSER THAN THIS.

SHFF SHFF SHFF
...
OH.
THAT'S CLOSE ENOUGH.
← Weak
I'M TOTALLY CON-FUSED.
THAT'S UNDER-STAND-ABLE!
IT'S JUST ... I PROB-ABLY ...
...SMELL RIGHT NOW.

DID YOU FaRT?
I DID NOT.
That's not what I meant.
I'VE GOTTEN REALLY SWEATY AND FILTHY.
I HAVEN'T HAD A BATH...
...SO MY HAIR IS...
THAT'S WHAT YOU'RE WORRIED ABOUT?
I REPEAT, THAT'S WHAT YOU'RE WORRIED ABOUT?!
UH...
WE'VE SPENT TONS OF TIME BEING FILTHY AND UNABLE TO TAKE A BATH ANYWHERE!
THIS IS JUST LIKE ALWAYS!
That's true, but...
IT'S EXTRA BAD THIS TIME!
NO, "EXTRA BAD" WAS WHEN WE WERE IN FIRE TRIBE TERRITORY!
YOU WERE COM-PLETELY GRIMY WHEN YOU—
AaGH! DON'T SaY iT OUT LOUD!

LOOK, IT DOESN'T BOTHER ME AND WE'RE BOTH IN THE SAME BOAT, SO WHAT'S THE BIG DEAL?
Come on, sit down.
PAT PAT
Y-YEAH...
I'LL STAY OVER HERE...
TUG TUG TUG TUG
I SAID IT DOESN'T BOTHER ME! YOU'RE BEING SUCH A PAIN!
NO, IT REALLY WILL BOTHER YOU!
I'M TELLING YOU IT'S FINE!
TUG TUG TUG TUG TUG TUG
OR AM I THE ONE WHO'S SMELLY?
NO, YOU SMELL FINE!
I don't mind.
WELL, HOW YOU SMELL IS OKAY TOO!
NO, IT'S NOT!
I CAN'T BELIEVE YOU'RE PULLING AS HARD AS ME! THAT'S AMAZING!
Did you gain dragon power somewhere?

OH, FOR—!
FWMP

SLUMP
HAK...
LET... GO...
SHK SHK
IF I LET GO, YOU'LL TAKE IT AS EVIDENCE THAT YOU REEK.
NO! YOU DON'T HAVE TO ENDURE THIS! REALLY!
I'M NOT "ENDURING" ANYTHING.
WELL...
I'VE ENDURED PLENTY OF OTHER THINGS, THOUGH.
JOLT
WHAT OTHER THINGS?!

SQUEEZE
H...
HAK...
HM...?
J-JUST...
...DON'T PUT YOUR FACE BY MY HAIR.
AH.
OKAY, FINE.

"Okay"?
YOU'RE NOT LISTENING AT ALL!
MY EARS AREN'T WORKING WELL RIGHT NOW.
I was hearing things earlier.
HAK.
YOU'RE JUST MESSING AROUND, AREN'T YOU?
NO, I'M NOT.
MY...
MY HEART FEELS LIKE IT'S GOING TO EXPLODE.

LET GO OF ME, OKAY?
IT'S FINE.
YOU SMELL SO NICE, YOUNG LADY.
IMITATING ZENO WILL NOT HELP, YOUNG FELLOW!
Contagious
Heh heh...

YOUR EYE-LID...
HUH?
IT'S SWOL-LEN.
AND YOUR LEG'S IN-JURED.
IT'S ALL RIGHT.
...
DON'T APOLOGIZE, OKAY? IT'S NOT YOUR FAULT.
...
HAK?
YOU'RE ...
...AWFULLY COOL, YOU KNOW.

WHAT? REAL-LY?
THE COOLEST GIRL I'VE EVER MET.
HUH—?! OH, THAT MAKES ME SO HAPPY!
I'LL KEEP IT UP!
PLEASE DON'T.
BUT YOU DON'T PRAISE ME THAT OFTEN!
NOW I'M MOTI-VATED!
WHATEVER YOU'RE MOTIVATED TO DO, PLEASE DON'T.
AND NOW SUDDENLY YOU'RE ALL WORRIED ABOUT YOUR LOOKS, LIKE SOME GIRL.
I *am* a girl.
YOU CAN NEVER BE TOO BEAUTIFUL.

This time around, I finished my storyboard unusually fast. We haven't had a Hak and Yona story in a while. But as I was having fun drawing, there were earthquakes in the middle of the night and I had to stop working. It was really difficult to get back to drawing again. On 3/16, there were levels 3 to 6 quakes all through the night. My house was a mess. I stood outside until morning. Thankfully, my family and my home got through it okay, but some of my friends weren't so lucky. There were people all over Kumamoto who were injured. Right now, I'm eating produce from Kumamoto to support the recovery effort. Thank you for all the messages and letters of encouragement!

TALKING TO SU-WON ALWAYS MADE ME SO HAPPY.
I ENJOYED IT SO MUCH...
I LOOKED FORWARD TO IT.
WHEREAS...
...WHEN I'M WITH HAK...
...IT'S A LITTLE DIFFERENT.
I FEEL LIKE I CAN'T REALLY BREATHE.
I GET TOO NERVOUS TO EVEN SAY ANYTHING.
BUT...
...I STILL WANT...
...TO BE RIGHT THERE WITH HIM.
HOW HAVE I BEEN ACTING IN FRONT OF HIM?

WHAT MATTERS MOST...
...IS THAT YOU'RE SAFE.
I DON'T KNOW WHAT GOT INTO ME THAT I THOUGHT IT WAS OKAY TO LEAVE YOU WITH TSUBARU. WE'D JUST MET HER, AND IN A TOWN WHERE WE'D HEARD PEOPLE WERE DISAP-PEARING...
I CAN'T BELIEVE I WAS SO NAIVE.
IT'S NO ONE'S FAULT.
YOU'D SUFFER MORE BEING WARY OF...
...PEOPLE WHO ARE KIND TO YOU.

NO MATTER HOW MANY TIMES I'M BETRAYED, I'LL NEVER, EVER STOP TRUSTING YOU.
PLEASE MAKE SAFETY YOUR PRIORITY, EVEN IF IT MAKES YOU SUFFER.
I'LL BE CARE-FUL.

HAK...
YOU'VE OBEYED MY FATHER'S ORDERS SO FAITH-FULLY.
WHEN THE TIME COMES...
...MY INTENTION IS TO...
...FREE YOU FROM THAT.

WHAT'LL I DO?
WHEN THAT TIME DOES COME...
...I'M NOT SURE...
...I'LL BE ABLE TO LET YOU GO.
CHAPTER 123 / THE END

THAT OLD MAN'S PRIZED RICE WINE SURE IS TASTY.
BONUS CHAPTER: FROM GOOD MORNING TO GOOD NIGHT
THAT'S ALL YOU HAVE TO SAY AFTER GETTING ALL THIS?

HE SAID HE'D GIVE ME RICE WINE IF I BEAT HIM AT ARM WRESTLING.
IT WAS FUN FOR A SECOND, BUT THEN IT WAS JUST EMBARRASSING TO SEE.
It was over in a flash.
WE DON'T OFTEN GET TO DO THIS, HAK.
WANT A REAL CHALLENGE?
TO SEE WHO COLLAPSES FIRST?
WHAT'LL YOU DO IF I WIN?
THE LOSER HAS TO DO ANYTHING THE WINNER SAYS.
How's that?
Oh?
"ANYTHING," HUH?
Hmm?
A CHALLENGE? I'LL DO IT TOO.
ZENO TOO!
Join us, Blue Dragon.

DON'T DO IT. THERE'S NO WAY YOU CAN BEAT HAK OR JAEHA.
YOU NEVER KNOW UNLESS YOU TRY.
THAT'S NOT TRUE.
THAT'S THE SPIRIT. TRY EVERYTHING AT LEAST ONCE!
YOU'RE JUST EGGING HIM ON BECAUSE YOU THINK YOU'LL BEAT HIM.
HOW ABOUT YOU, YUN?
DON'T BE RIDICULOUS.
I'LL MAKE SOME SNACKS.
WE APPRECIATE EVERYTHING YOU DO, MOM.
DON'T CALL ME THAT.
ARM WRESTLING, HUH? I WOULD HAVE LIKED TO PARTICIPATE.
Ugh...
IF YOU HAD, YOU WOULD'VE BROKEN YOUR OPPONENT'S ARM.
YOU KNOW, SOMETIMES I WONDER ...
... WHICH IS STRONGER.
WHAT DO YOU MEAN?

YOUR ARM, GIJA...
...OR JAEHA'S LEG.
...
...
SWP
SWP
WHY DID YOU TURN AWAY? LOOK INTO MY EYES, JAEHA.
I'M... FEELING A BIT DIZZY.
Maybe I'm drunk?
GRAB
I RE-MEMBER HEARING A LEGEND.
LONG, LONG AGO, THERE WAS A SPEAR THAT COULD PIERCE ANY SHIELD AND A SHIELD THAT COULD BLOCK ANY SPEAR.

WHEN THOSE TWO ULTIMATE WEAPONS CLASHED, THEY WERE BOTH OBLITERATED.
ALL RIGHT! LET'S SEE WHICH OF US IS DE-STROYED.
TWITCH TWITCH
AH... NO?
STOP, GIJA. I HAVE NO INTENTION OF FIGHTING YOU, AND I DEFINITELY DON'T WANT TO BE DESTROYED.
I DIDN'T SAY ANYTHING ABOUT KILLING EACH OTHER. I JUST WANT YOU TO TRY BLOCKING MY FIST.
LURCH
YOUR FIST COULD KILL PEOPLE!
OKAY, FINE. BUT LET'S HAVE A DRINK BEFORE WE DO IT, OKAY?
GLUB GLUB
OKAY.
ZZZ...
SWFF
ALL RIGHT, ONE DOWN.

SIP
NOW, NEXT UP...
WOW, SINHA, YOU SURE CAN DRINK.
Deftly slipped Sinha's mask off
POINK
ARE YOU STILL ALIVE?
SKRIK
JAEHA... I CAN SEE...
SKRIK SKRIK SKRIK SKRIK
...YOUR HEART.
Okay, never mind.
WE'LL LET SINHA BE.
SINHA, DRINK OVER HERE.
LEAVE HIM ALONE!

SO THAT JUST LEAVES ME, HAK AND ZENO...
SIP SIP
So tasty.
SIP SIP
HAK... WE MIGHT BE UP AGAINST AN IMPRESSIVE OPPONENT.
HMM?

GRIN
OH!
ZENO, DON'T TELL ME...
Ha Ha! THAT'S RIGHT!
NO MATTER HOW MUCH ZENO DRINKS, IT ONLY MAKES HIM TIPSY FOR A LITTLE WHILE. HE CAN NEVER GET WASTED.
HE'S THE STRONGEST DRINKER IN THE WORLD!
HE'S UNDEFEATABLE!
WE'RE NOT COUNTING YOU, ZENO.
Aww. No fun.
IT'S FINE IF ZENO JOINS IN!
LOOK, YOUR HIGHNESS, HE'S...

ANOTHER SHOT FOR ME!
HOLD ON, YOU'RE PARTICI-PATING?!
YOU WERE AS QUIET AS SINHA. I THOUGHT YOU WERE ASLEEP.
I'M WIDE-AWAKE.
SLUMP
NOW YOU'RE ASLEEP.
AM NOT.
GO TO BED.
HAK ...
YES?
HEY, HAK...
UH-HUH?
WHEN ...

...IT COMES TO YOU, I...
WHAT WAS THAT ABOUT?
HON- ESTLY ...
ZZZ...

IF YOU WON'T CARRY HER, MAYBE I WILL.
...
JERK.
IF YOU LEAVE THIS AREA, YOU FORFEIT!
Ugh.
GOTTA CLEAR MY HEAD.
...
NOW THEN, WHAT SHOULD WE ORDER HAK TO DO?
WHAT ARE YOU SMILING ABOUT, ZENO?

Heh...
WATCHING YOU TWO IS SO HEART-WARMING.
OH, SHUT UP.
YOU AND I ARE THE ONLY ONES LEFT...
ZZZ...
WAIT, WHAT? YOU'RE SO CAREFREE.
EVEN THOUGH YOU'RE PRETTY SOBER, YOU WENT TO SLEEP WHEN YOU GOT TIRED.
ZZZ...
EVERY-ONE'S ASLEEP.
I GUESS THAT MEANS I WIN?
WHAT SHOULD THE WINNER ...
...ASK THE LOSERS TO DO?

I CAN'T THINK OF ANY-THING.
I COULDN'T WISH...
...FOR ANYTHING MORE.
IT'S MORN-ING!
WAKE UP!

THROB
THROB
M-MORNING, YUN...
COME TO THINK OF IT, YOU DISAPPEARED HALFWAY THROUGH...
CARRIED THE OTHER THREE DRAGONS TO THE TENT, PUT THEM TO BED AND DRANK BY HIMSELF
STAYED WITH YONA AND COULDN'T SLEEP
Huh?
I CLEARED AWAY THE DISHES AND WATCHED THE FIRE.
ONCE I GOT UP, I DID SOME FORAGING AND COOKED BREAKFAST, AND I'M DOING LAUNDRY.
IF YOU HAVE ANYTHING THAT NEEDS MENDING, GO GET IT.
THE WIN-NER!
HUH?
THE WIN-NER!
The amazing Yun for 2016!
WHAT ?
NO OBJEC-TIONS!
WHAT ?!
EVERYONE, DO WHAT-EVER YUN SAYS!
BONUS CHAPTER / THE END

*On calligraphy sheet: Smile

Volume 21 went on sale in Japan during the summer. The special edition with the OAD (original animation DVD) and Zeno on the cover went on sale during the winter. This picture of Yun on the cover looks like it's from autumn. The picture of Gija, Yona and Sinha on the back cover looks like it's from summertime. Yona is writing her first calligraphy of the year here...

—Mizuho Kusanagi

Born on February 3 in Kumamoto Prefecture in Japan, Mizuho Kusanagi began her professional manga career with *Yoiko no Kokoroe* (The Rules of a Good Child) in 2003. Her other works include *NG Life*, which was serialized in *Hana to Yume* and *The Hana to Yume* magazines and published by Hakusensha in Japan. *Yona of the Dawn* was adapted into an anime in 2014.

YONA OF THE DAWN

VOL.21
Shojo Beat Edition

STORY AND ART BY
MIZUHO KUSANAGI

English Adaptation/Ysabet Reinhardt MacFarlane
Translation/JN Productions
Touch-Up Art & Lettering/Lys Blakeslee
Design/Philana Chen
Editor/Amy Yu

Printed in the U.S.A.

Published by VIZ Media, LLC
P.O. Box 77010
San Francisco, CA 94107

10 9 8 7 6 5 4 3 2 1
First printing, December 2019

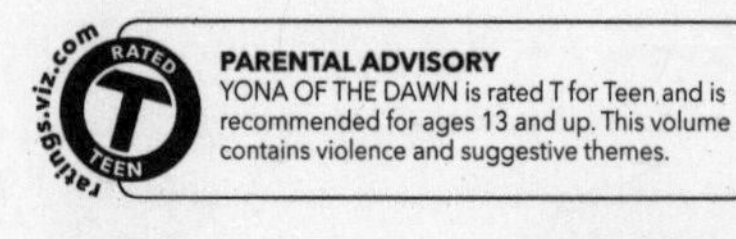

viz.com shojobeat.com